Desert Babies

Kathy Darling
Photographs by Tara Darling

Walker and Company
New York

Appreciation is due to The Living Desert of Palm Desert, California—whose celebration of desert life is a model of community involvement. Thanks especially to Susie Kirby for allowing us to photograph animals from the collection.

Thank you to Paul and Brenda Zimmerman for letting us photograph the baby emus bred at Hammercreek Farm, Lititz, Pennsylvania.

To Clark Moorten of Moorten Botanical Gardens in Palm Springs, California, who watches over the baby tortoises that live among his cactuses.

To the Miami Metro Zoo for a bird's-eye view of young vulture life.

To the Animal Kingdom of Bordentown, New Jersey, which allowed us to share their coyote pup.

To Brad, Karen, and Megan Bonar, who have provided a sanctuary for the little caracal we photographed at Black Pine Animal Park in Albion, Indiana.

Really sincere thanks to Clyde Peeling, rattlesnake wrangler extraordinaire, who protected me while I photographed his deadly charges at Reptiland in Allenwood, Pennsylvania.

To the Catskill Game Farm, which has provided an oasis for the baby camels we photographed there.

And to real-life Spidermen, Rob Cherico, chief web surfer of Itchy By Nature in Pompano Beach, Florida, and Frank Somma of New York. We can see how tarantulas like the ones we photographed can get under your skin!

First published in the United States of America in 1997 by Walker Publishing Company, Inc.

Published simultaneously in Canada by Thomas Allen & Son Canada, Limited, Markham, Ontario

Library of Congress Cataloging-in-Publication Data
Darling, Kathy.
Desert Babies / Kathy Darling; photographs by Tara Darling.
p.   cm.
Summary: Photographs and brief text describe a variety of baby animals, some of whom are endangered, who make their homes in the desert.
ISBN 0-8027-8479-8 (hardcover). –ISBN 0-8027-8480-1 (reinforced)
1. Desert animals–Infancy–Juvenile literature. [1. Desert animals. 2. Animals–infancy.
3. Endangered species.] I. Darling, Tara, ill. II. Title.
QL 116.D3 1997
591.909'54–dc20   96-32912
CIP
AC
Map on page 3 and desert and endangered species icons throughout the book by Dennis O'Brien.
Artwork on page 32 by Linda Howard and Elizabeth Sieferd.
Book design by Marva J. Martin.
Printed in Hong Kong
2 4 6 8 10 9 7 5 3 1

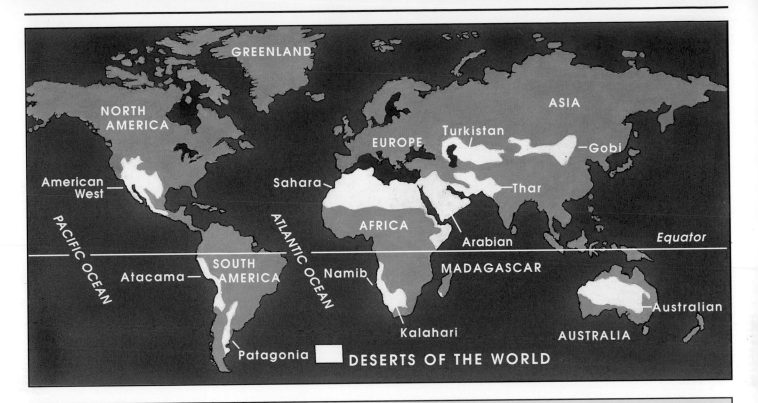

These symbols appear throughout the book and represent the landscapes of the desert that each animal inhabits. For more information about these landscapes turn to "About the Desert" on the last page of the book.

PAN

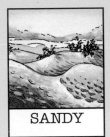

SANDY

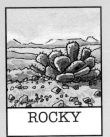

ROCKY

The desert is not the land that nature forgot. It's hot. It's dry. And it's a hard place to make a living. But more than 5,000 species of plants and animals have made desert lands their permanent home.

Join our reading caravan and trek across the burning sands of the Sahara, the pebbly outback of Australia, and the cactus forests of the United States' own Mojave Desert in search of the most adorable babies in the badlands. Of course, in such harsh lands there are bound to be a few tough toddlers too. Come and meet them all.

SANDY

Camel

Some camels have two humps. Others have one. A newborn camel doesn't have a hump at all. It is born without those lumps on its back, which are places for storing not water but fat.

This month-old calf (facing page) is getting fat on its mother's milk. A fat camel isn't fat anywhere but in its hump. It can keep cooler because its whole body isn't wrapped in fat.

The desert's biggest animals, camels are specialists at surviving in hot, dry, dusty places. They have not one but two rows of eyelashes to screen out blowing sand, and special muscles to close ears, nostrils, and lips. Big flat feet prevent the camel from sinking into the dunes.

Camel
(Bactrian Camel)

ENDANGERED
SPECIES

- Baby name: Calf
- Birthplace: Sand
- Birth size: 90 to 100 pounds, 5 feet tall
- Adult size: 1,600 to 1,800 pounds, 7 to 7 1/2 feet tall
- Littermates: None. Twins are possible but not common.
- Favorite food: A baby drinks a gallon of milk every day for a year and a half. After a few months it also begins to nibble on the desert plants its parents eat.
- Parent care: Mother feeds and protects her baby. Camels live in big groups called herds that are led by the oldest females.
- Enemies: Humans
- Home deserts: Gobi and Turkestan in Asia

SANDY

ROCKY

PAN

Caracal

This little kitten (facing page) will grow up to be a creep. And a sneak too. Adult caracals (right) hunt by creeping and sneaking.

They are very successful at it. That's because they are also great athletes. If there were Olympics for cats, caracals would win gold medals. This desert lynx, whose strange name means "black ear," is fast and agile enough to snatch a bird right out of the air. A two-week-old kitten like this one is too young for serious athletics, but it will grow up to be the best jumper in the cat family.

Caracal
(KAR-eh-kal)
(Desert Lynx)

ENDANGERED SPECIES

- Baby name: Kitten
- Birthplace: Hollow tree or underground burrow
- Birth size: 7 ounces
- Adult size: 35 to 55 pounds; 40 inches long plus a 10-inch tail
- Littermates: 1 to 3
- Favorite food: Babies drink milk. Adults eat the meat of birds, mice, and small antelope.
- Parent care: Mother provides total care. Baby stays with mother about a year.
- Enemies: Humans
- Home deserts: Asia, Middle East, and Africa

Gemsbok

Horns! Long, sharp horns. That's the first thing you notice about a gemsbok. Males have them. Females have them. And unlike other baby antelope, newborn gemsbok have them. Of course, they are only baby-sized horns. But gemsbok parents are fierce protectors and will use their big horns to keep their calf safe.

Gemsbok babies, like this two-month-old calf (facing page), are born in the spring so they can eat the green grass that grows only at that time of year.

Are unicorns real? When viewed from the side, the gemsbok appears to have a single horn. Could this antelope that lives in the driest places on Earth be the magical animal of fairy tales and legends?

Gemsbok
(Gemsbok Oryx)

- Baby name: Calf
- Birthplace: No special place
- Birth size: 25 pounds
- Adult size: 450 pounds, 4 feet at shoulder
- Littermates: None
- Favorite food: Babies drink milk for 4 months, then eat grass, plant roots, and melons.
- Parent care: Mother nurses and protects baby. Gemsbok live in groups called herds, and all adults protect young.
- Enemies: Desert lions, hyenas, jackals (babies only), and caracal (babies only)
- Home deserts: Southern Africa

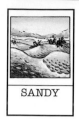

Mouse

Egyptian spiny mice have a very short childhood. Most baby mice are born blind, deaf, and naked. Not the spiny mouse. It alone comes into the world with its eyes wide open, able to hear, and wearing a coat of the porcupine-like hairs that give it its name.

In spite of their prickly fur, spiny mice live in groups and love to huddle together between rocks or in earth tunnels they sometimes share with gerbils.

By the time it is seven weeks old, a spiny mouse has grown to full size and is ready to be a mother or father.

Mouse
(Egyptian Spiny Mouse)

- Birthplace: Hole in the ground or crack between rocks
- Birth size: 1/2 ounce
- Adult size: 2 to 3 ounces, 3 inches long (about the same size as a house mouse)
- Littermates: Up to 6
- Favorite food: Babies drink milk for about a week. Then they eat seeds and leaves like their parents.
- Parent care: Mother cares for babies alone. Older females are nurse-helpers at the birth.
- Enemies: Caracal, fennec fox, snakes, big birds
- Home desert: Sahara of northern Africa

Quokka

Baby animals are always smaller than their parents. Some are a lot smaller. A newborn quokka, a kangaroo, is 5,000 times smaller than its mother. It's about the size of a grain of rice when it's born.

A tiny baby quokka stays in a pouch on its mother's stomach. When it gets a little bigger, the joey (that's what you call a baby kangaroo) will hop in and out of this handy carriage. Even when it is too big to be carried, like this six-month-old joey (facing page), it will stick its head inside the pouch to take a drink of milk.

Quokka
(KWAH-kuh)
(Short-tailed Kangaroo)

ENDANGERED SPECIES

- Baby name: Joey
- Birthplace: Under a bush
- Birth size: About as big as a grain of rice
- Adult size: 6 to 8 pounds
- Littermates: None
- Favorite food: Baby drinks milk. Adults eat leaves and grass.
- Parent care: Mother carries baby in pouch. Father does not help.
- Enemies: Feral house cats, foxes, birds of prey
- Home deserts: Mainland and small offshore islands of southwest Australia

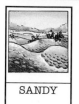

Uromastyx

If you lived in the Sahara Desert, you could use a spiny-tailed lizard to tell the temperature. The skin of this living thermometer changes color with the weather. When it is cool, a male uromastyx is black. But on a sizzling hot day, which is most of the time in the Sahara, he is a bright yellow color. Females and babies of either sex are a dull brown all the time.

Although uromastyx can stand sand temperatures over 150 degrees Fahrenheit, sometimes the desert is too hot even for them. With powerful claws, a uromastyx can dig a cool underground burrow and block the entrance with a spiny tail that is every bit as dangerous as it looks.

Uromastyx
(YOU-ROW-mass-sticks)
(Spiny-tailed Lizard)

ENDANGERED
SPECIES

- Birthplace: Sandy nest
- Birth size: 3 inches long when it hatches from the egg
- Adult size: 12 ounces, 14 inches long (Males are bigger than females.)
- Littermates: 20 to 30
- Favorite food: Dates, flowers, and plants. Primarily a vegetarian, this lizard occasionally eats insects.
- Parent care: None
- Enemies: Birds of prey, snakes, jackals, caracal
- Home desert: Sahara of northern Africa

ROCKY

SANDY

PAN

Coyote

Yip, yip, yip, and yowl is the coyote version of "Home on the Range." At night the little song dog can be heard singing in just about any desert in the American West. The home range of wolves and wild dogs is shrinking in most parts of the world, but the coyote's territory just keeps getting bigger.

Brains are the reason. A toddler like this six-week-old puppy (facing page) is already learning how to outsmart other animals—including humans. The coyote's real home is the desert, and from the salt flats to the snowy high country, it can find food there. But it can also live right in the middle of towns, wiggling its wily way into the backyards of America.

Coyote

- Baby name: Puppy
- Birthplace: Hollow log, burrow, or rock den
- Birth size: 1 pound
- Adult size: 25 to 30 pounds, 20 inches tall
- Littermates: 4 to 9, but 6 is average.
- Favorite food: Puppies drink milk. Adults eat small rodents, birds, and reptiles.
- Parent care: Mother takes complete care of the puppies for the first few weeks. After a month, when pups get teeth, both parents bring food.
- Enemies: Humans, mountain lions, badgers
- Home deserts: Desert and semidesert regions of North and Central America

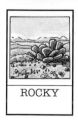

ROCKY

Emu

"Come to Daddy!" calls the father emu when the weather is very hot. He spreads his stubby wings and makes shade for his striped chicks. On cold nights he stretches his wings across the sand and invites the babies to cozy up under his feathers.

His wings aren't any good for flying. That's okay, though. An emu can run faster than any of its enemies. Long legs and tough toes whiz him across the Australian outback at forty miles an hour. That's faster than a horse!

Emu chicks can't run that fast, so their hundred-pound daddy uses his strong legs to protect them. With a loud cry of "E-moo," he delivers a karate kick to anything that is foolish enough to threaten his babies.

Emu
(E-moo)

- Baby name: Chick
- Birthplace: Ground nest made of grass, leaves, bark, or twigs
- Birth size: 1 pound, 6 inches
- Adult size: 120 pounds, 6 feet tall (Females are slightly bigger than males.)
- Littermates: 7 to 9
- Favorite food: Grass, leaves, flowers, fruits, seeds, and some insects. Babies especially like caterpillars and grasshoppers.
- Parent care: Father sits on eggs from several mothers and takes care of chicks for up to 18 months. Mothers do not help.
- Enemies: Dingos, birds of prey, especially buzzards, which break the eggs
- Home desert: Australian outback

Lemur

For a long time, people thought the spiny deserts of Madagascar were haunted. They heard spooky howls and eerie wails. When they saw pale white forms leaping about, they called them *lemurs*, which means "ghost."

The "ghosts" weren't ghosts at all but beautiful animals that are now called sifaka lemurs. Sifakas, like this adult (right), are great leapers. From a standstill they can jump up to thirty feet sideways, forward, or backward. A newborn sifaka hangs onto its mother's belly fur and gets a wild ride. Bigger babies get to ride piggyback.

Lemur
(Sifaka Lemur)
(see FAHK uh LEE mer)

ENDANGERED SPECIES

- Birthplace: Spiny tree or ground
- Birth size: 1 1/2 pounds
- Adult size: 10 pounds, 1 1/2 feet tall with a 2-foot-long tail
- Littermates: None
- Favorite food: Leaves, fruit, and flowers
- Parent care: Baby is cared for by mother only.
- Enemies: Snakes, hawks, and a catlike animal called a fossa
- Home desert: Southern Madagascar, a large island near Africa

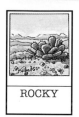

ROCKY

Snake

Rattlesnakes make music but they can't hear their own song. They're deaf.

The little knobs at the end of a rattlesnake's tail are called bells, clickers, buzzers, whirrers, or rattles. But no matter what they are called, people pay attention to the warning noise they make. Rattlesnakes are dangerous. Even newborn rattlers have fangs that are armed with a deadly poison.

With only two rattles, this month-old baby (facing page) can't make much noise. It takes eight buttons to shake up a really loud sound. Rattlesnakes add another button each time they change their skin for a bigger size, and it takes about two years to become a loud musician.

Snake
(Western Diamondback Rattlesnake)

- Birthplace: Mother's den
- Birth size: About an ounce, 8 to 13 inches long
- Adult size: Sometimes over 20 pounds, 5 feet or longer (The record is a 23-pounder that was 6 feet long.)
- Littermates: 3 to 24, although 8 or 10 is more common
- Favorite food: Small animals. Newborn rattlers are big enough to eat a full-grown mouse or a baby bird.
- Parent care: Babies are born alive, not hatched from eggs like most snakes. After birth, mother and father give no care.
- Enemies: Humans, birds of prey—especially the roadrunner—skunks, snake-eating snakes, and pigs
- Home deserts: Mojave, Sonoran, and other places in the American West

Tarantula

Tarantulas are spiders that defend themselves with a most unusual weapon—itching powder. When threatened, they kick special hairs off their rear end at an attacker. Poison in these hairs causes horrible itching if it gets in an animal's eyes or mouth or on naked skin.

This four-month-old spiderling (facing page) doesn't have any of the itchy hairs. It will be a few more months before it has the red color that signals the growth of the fuzzy weapons.

Tarantula
(Mexican Red Knee Tarantula)

- Baby name: Spiderling
- Birthplace: Wherever mother is
- Birth size: 1/3 inch from front to back leg tip
- Adult size: 6 inches from front to back leg tip
- Littermates: 300 to 800
- Favorite food: Babies eat insects; adults eat insects, small lizards, and mice.
- Parent care: Mother carries eggs in a silken case and protects them. Once they hatch, the spiderlings are on their own.
- Enemies: Lizards, snakes, wasps
- Home deserts: Mexico

PAN

Nilgai

Nilgai calves are almost always twins. They look like miniature copies of their mother. The cow and her calves are tawny brown with white markings on the legs and face. These two-month-old babies might not recognize their father. They don't look much like him. A nilgai bull is blue-gray with a black beard and a pair of sharp horns on his head.

If a calf is a male, it will grow up to look like its daddy. When he gets to be six months old, you will be able to see tiny antelope horns beginning to sprout on his head.

Nilgai
(Nil-guy)
(Nilgai Antelope)

- Baby name: Calf
- Birthplace: No special place
- Birth size: 40 to 50 pounds, 2 feet at shoulder
- Adult size: 500 pounds, 4 1/2 feet at shoulder
- Littermates: Usually 1
- Favorite food: Calves drink milk. Adults eat grasses and leaves.
- Parent care: Mother takes complete care of the calf.
- Enemies: Humans and packs of Indian wild dogs called dhole
- Home desert: Thar of Asia

Tortoise

The desert tortoise always carries a bottle of water with it. A special sack under its shell can hold a six-month supply of the life-giving liquid. Half the tortoise's weight is often stored water.

A newborn tortoise's shell is not strong enough to support a very big water sack. It is softer and thinner than your fingernail. Not until seven of the hundred years of its life have gone by will the desert tortoise's shell be tough enough to protect it from its enemies.

This adult desert tortoise (above) lives life in the slow lane even compared to other turtles. For nine months of every year it sleeps underground, surviving on stored food and water.

Tortoise
(American Desert Tortoise)

ENDANGERED SPECIES

- Baby name: Hatchling
- Birthplace: Eggs are laid in a funnel-shaped nest, often dug near the entrance to the mother's burrow.
- Birth size: Eggs are the size of a Ping Pong ball. The shell of a hatchling measures 2 inches across.
- Adult size: Shell measures up to 14 inches across.
- Littermates: 1 to 11
- Favorite food: Cactus and other desert plants
- Parent care: None
- Enemies: Humans and their automobiles, bobcats, mountain lions, coatimundi, cacomistle, and birds of prey
- Home desert: Mojave in Southwest United States

PAN

Vulture

Vultures eat the most disgusting, yucky things you can imagine. They love decaying meat. Something dead and crawling with worms is, to them, just yummy. One reason they can eat such stinky stuff is because, like most birds, they have no sense of smell. The rotten food is washed down with equally gross drinks. This two-month-old chick (facing page) gets regular deliveries of spit dribbled down its throat!

Flying in lazy circles high over the desert, vultures can spot snacks miles away. With the help of warm air rising off the sand, the searching birds soar for hours without flapping their wings.

Vulture
(Whitebacked Vulture)

- Baby name: Chick
- Birthplace: Huge nest made of twigs and lined with leaves
- Birth size: 3 ounces
- Adult size: 10 pounds, 7-foot wingspan
- Littermates: None
- Favorite food: Meat—fresh or rotten
- Parent care: Both parents sit on the egg and help feed the chick.
- Enemies: Snakes, other birds of prey
- Home deserts: Southern Africa

About the Desert

When you think of deserts, you probably think of sand. But less than 20 percent of the Earth's deserts are sandy. In these lands, the shifting sand is like a grainy sea. Driven by high winds, it moves across the land in waves like a slow-motion ocean. Huge piles of it, called dunes, can rise over a thousand feet from the desert floor.

Another desert landscape is the broken, baked surface called a pan. Made of hard-packed mud or salt, pans are the hottest, driest places on Earth.

Most desert lands, however, are covered with small pebbles or stones. Sometimes called gibber, these rocky places are usually dotted with scrubby plants or cactus and rocks carved into strange shapes by the wind.

A desert is a place where heat, cold, and lack of water all make life difficult. It is also a place where life, with its talent for survival, has responded in marvelous ways. Babies, for instance, are produced only after a rain has fallen and the desert blooms. Desert dwellers are quick to take advantage of these rare times of plenty by storing food and water. Some survive by sleeping during the summer (aestivating) or in the cold months (hibernating). A few even do both. There are animals that don't drink—not ever. And dieters that can stretch a meal for an entire year.

The remarkable babies of the desert can live where we cannot. They can fight and beat the heat, and the cold, and the dry conditions. What they cannot beat is human interference in their fragile ecosystem.